ANIMALS GROWING UP™

HOW DOLPHINS GROW UP

Enslow Publishing
101 W. 23rd Street
Suite 240
New York, NY 10011
USA

enslow.com

Linda Bozzo

WORDS TO KNOW

calf A baby dolphin.

carnivores Animals that eat meat.

mammals Warm-blooded animals that breathe air, have backbones and hair, and produce milk for their young.

mate To come together to have babies.

nurse To drink milk from the mother.

pods Groups of dolphins.

predators Animals that kill and eat other animals to live.

prey An animal that is killed and eaten by another animal.

social Living together in groups.

species A group of the same kind of living thing that has the same scientific name.

CONTENTS

DOLPHINS AROUND THE WORLD

There are more than 40 different species, or kinds, of dolphins. The largest is the killer whale. It is also called an orca. A well-known dolphin is the bottlenose.

Dolphins live in oceans and rivers around the world.

A bottlenose dolphin swims in the ocean.

5

DOLPHINS MATE

Dolphins mate, or come together to have babies, all year. When it is time to give birth, the mother will swim away from the other dolphins.

A mother dolphin rubs faces with her baby.

FAST FACT

A dolphin usually gives birth to only one baby. Giving birth to twins is uncommon.

BABY DOLPHINS

A baby dolphin is called a calf. Calves are most often born tail first and underwater. The calf swims to the top for its first breath.

Calves are usually darker in color than adult dolphins.

A mother and her one-day-old calf swim along the surface of the water.

DOLPHINS ARE MAMMALS

Like most mammals, dolphins give birth to live young. A mother dolphin nurses, or feeds her calf milk. Calves are born with tiny hairs at the top of their mouths.

A calf's hair falls out within two weeks of birth. It does not grow any other hair for the rest of its life.

A calf nurses from its mother underwater. All mammal mothers make milk for their babies to drink.

SOCIAL ANIMALS

Dolphins are social animals. They live together in groups called pods. Mother dolphins form their own pods. They help each other feed and protect their calves.

A calf stays close to its mother as the pod swims. The other dolphins in the pod would protect the calf, too.

A DOLPHIN'S DIET

As dolphins grow up, they grow teeth. They start eating fish, squid, shrimp, and other seafood. Dolphins use their teeth to hold their prey. They do not chew their food.

Dolphins are **carnivores**, or meat-eating animals.

A six-month-old calf chomps down on a tasty fish.

15

DOLPHINS SPEAK

A mother dolphin calls her calf using her special whistle. A calf will form its own whistle around one month old. Dolphins also click, chirp, and scream to talk to each other.

A dolphin breathes through a blowhole on top of its head.

A dolphin's whistle is like a name. It's how they tell each other apart.

17

WATCH OUT!

Lucky for dolphins, they have very few predators. This means not many animals are able to eat dolphins. But large sharks and orcas have attacked small, young, or sick dolphins.

Dolphins can swim faster than almost any animal that would try to hunt them.

FAST FACT

Dolphins swim too fast for most sharks to catch them!

LEAVING MOTHER

During its first year of life, a calf stays close to its mother. After three or more years, calves join other young dolphins that have left their mothers.

FAST FACT

The sense of touch is very important between calves and their mothers.

A calf touches its mother with its chin. It makes the bond between them stronger.

21

A LONG LIFE

Orcas may live 50 to 80 years or more in the wild. Some bottlenose dolphins live 20 years or less. Others can live as long as 45 to 50 years.

An orca, the largest species of dolphin, shows off its teeth.

FAST FACT

Scientists can guess a dolphin's age by looking at a slice of a tooth and counting the layers.

LEARN MORE

Books

American Museum of Natural History. *Baby Dolphin's First Swim*. New York, NY: Sterling Children's Books, 2017.

Clay, Kathryn. *Bottlenose Dolphins*. North Mankato, MN: Pebble Books, 2019.

Hansen, Grace. *Dolphins*. North Mankato, MN: Capstone, 2017.

Websites

Dolphin Research Center
dolphins.org/kids_dolphin_facts
Read fun facts about dolphins.

National Geographic Kids: Bottlenose Dolphins
kids.nationalgeographic.com/animals/bottlenose-dolphin
Dive deeper into dolphins with videos, facts, and photos.

INDEX

Published in 2020 by Enslow Publishing, LLC.
101 W. 23rd Street, Suite 240, New York, NY 10011

Copyright © 2020 by Enslow Publishing, LLC

Library of Congress Cataloging-in-Publication Data

Names: Bozzo, Linda, author.
Title: How dolphins grow up / Linda Bozzo.
Description: New York : Enslow Publishing, 2020. | Series: Animals growing up | Audience: Grades K to 3. | Includes bibliographical references and index.
Identifiers: LCCN 2018041871| ISBN 9781978507197 (library bound) | ISBN 9781978508194 (pbk.) | ISBN 9781978508200 (6 pack)
Subjects: LCSH: Dolphins—Development—Juvenile literature. | Dolphins—Infancy—Juvenile literature.
Classification: LCC QL737.C432 B69 2019 | DDC 599.53/1392—dc23
LC record available at https://lccn.loc.gov/2018041871

Printed in the United States of America

To Our Readers: We have done our best to make sure all websites in this book were active and appropriate when we went to press. However, the author and the publisher have no control over and assume no liability for the material available on those websites or on any websites they may link to. Any comments or suggestions can be sent by email to customerservice@enslow.com.

Photo Credits: Cover, p. 1 vkilikov/Shutterstock.com; p. 5 R. Maximiliane/Shutterstock.com; p. 7 Jeff Rotman/Photolibrary/Getty Images; pp. 9, 15 Wild Horizon/Universal Images Group/Getty Images; p. 11 Hiroya Minakuchi/Minden Pictures/Getty Images; pp. 13, 19, interior backgrounds Willyam Bradberry/Shutterstock.com; pp. 17, 21 Eco/Universal Images Group/Getty Images; p. 23 Christian Musat/Shutterstock.com.